RAGAS FROM THE PERIPHERY

R A G A S

FROM THE PERIPHERY

. . .

PHINDER DULAI

ARSENAL PULP PRESS

VANCOUVER

ARSENAL PULP PRESS
100-1062 Homer Street
Vancouver, B.C.
Canada V6B 2W9

The publisher gratefully acknowledges the assistance of the Canada Council and the Cultural Services Branch, B.C. Ministry of Small Business, Recreation and Culture.

Some of these poems have been previously published in *Ankur, Canadian Ethnic Studies, the Toronto South Asian Review,* and *Rungh.*

Printed and bound in Canada

CANADIAN CATALOGUING IN PUBLICATION DATA:
Dulai, Phinder, 1967-
  Ragas from the periphery

  Poems.
  isbn 1-55152-021-4

  I. Title.
PS8557.U49R33 1995   C811'.54   C95-910232-9
PR9199.3.D84R33 1995

CONTENTS

ACKNOWLEDGEMENTS

Neither the manuscript nor this book would have found the light of day had it not been for some friends who have quietly helped me along in my years of doubt and failure.

To my friends in the academy: Chin Bannerjee, Fred Candelaria, Ralph Maud, Harjot Oberoi, Malcolm Page, and Uma Pamaeswaran—a humble word of thanks for moving mountains in front of me.

To my manuscript readers and fellow writers: Sadhu Binning, Surjeet Kalsey, Cameron McAlpine, Rajinderpal S. Pal, Ajmer Rode, Michael Roth, and Michael Turner, for their diversity of criticism, for nurturing me to make this book the best one I could write, and for helping me along when times got tough.

The *Ankur* magazine meetings were ones of clarity and vision; it was the only magazine at the time that would publish my work in Canada. I thank the editorial collective: Nirmaljeet, Harji, Farhat, Pindy, Jeevan, Sital, Amanpal, Anju, Sukhwant, and Sunera, for gently nudging me along, and always offering a hand of support.

To my friends at *Rungh* magazine: Zool Suleman and Sherazad Jamal, thank you for supporting my work, and being there to do whatever you could to better this poet's path.

This work would also not have gotten off the ground had it not been for the generous support of the Canada Council through the Explorations and Writing Programs.

To my editor/publisher Brian Lam and the staff at Arsenal Pulp Press, for believing in this work, and offering a keen eye for detail. My gratitude is endless.

And finally to my three loves, Jane, Natasha, and Nadya, for allowing me the time to complete this work and inspiring the muse within me.

LETTING THE IMAGE FORM THE SOUND

To some the title of this collection is obvious in its implications, but vague to those unfamiliar with the term *ragas*. The raga is a melodic musical composition that primarily defines the classical musical tradition of India. Ragas are always played in accordance with the time of day—morning, afternoon, or evening—and also impart a central emotion—sadness, anger, joy, love, melancholy. In this context, this collection is made up of poems of emotion, about the solitary experience of a writer struggling to find an audience. The *periphery* focusses on where this literary activity is taking place, namely on the margins of contemporary society.

This collection also serves as my polemic in the midst of the English literary tradition as it relates to the creation and canonization of a Canadian literary identity. This does not, however, overlook the very real education I received as a student of literature. I grew up reading modernist writers such as Virginia Woolf, T.S. Eliot, James Joyce, and Henry Miller. Peripheral to this canon has always been my love of the contemporary literary scene which includes writers such as Hanif Kureishi, Salman Rushdie, Rohinton Mistry, Michael Ondaatje, and Toni Morrison, to name a few.

I say I am first and foremost a South Asian writer—and within this exists my Canadian identity—because I cannot deny the social and political context in which I find myself today. I would be lying if I said that somehow these *Ragas* were not shaped by political and social movements that took place during the 1980s, and their effect on people's notions of what was validated and recognized as English literature and what was re-classified as world, or migrant, literature. Since then, all lines have become blurred and questionable, and world literature, once marginalized, now enjoys a truly global appeal.

Much like a raga's cycle, the poems in this collection are built upon the momentum and fluidity that carries the images as they are transported along this river of consciousness. Where they go, and what happens to them after the end of the poem, is up to the reader.

For Mani & Gian,
who gave birth to a poet

. . . I spend my time at the
the great work of preserving.
Memory, as well as fruit, is
being saved from the corruption
of the clocks. . . . Things—
even people—have a way of
leaking into each other. . . .
Likewise . . . the past has
dripped into me . . . so we
can't ignore it. . . . As history
pours out of my fissured body.
—SALMAN RUSHDIE, *Midnight's Children*

Every phrase and every sentence is an end and a
   beginning.
Every poem an epitaph. And any action
Is a step to the block, to the fire, down the sea's throat.
—T.S. ELIOT, *Little Gidding—The Four Quartets*

A RAGA FROM THE PERIPHERY

This middle point
Is it the least effective
or the colour of the core?

This peripheral line
Is it the border of hostility
or a distant coloured horizon?

So what of this heart!

Does it beat in time
or work on a six/8 rhythm?

The twilight brings
                    Te bea(dhin)g of te rhy(dhum)[1]:

                         - dhi dhum dhin
                           thikathum thikathum -

This song it sings.
Upon my divan I lie
at this hour I love
my beloved, Ah!
                    - my beloved is unto me
                      as a cluster of camphire -

NO!

                         - dhi dhum dhin -
                           this song it sings

Parvati pours into me
the beauty of her wisdom
hers is the sublime time

mine is the surrounding silence
my eyes angry and hard
commences
the hand
slaps the tablas drum

here the music shall begin.

1. Dhin/dhum—tala words—tablas
INDIAN MUSIC

ANGER

My anger is not
a solid ball of clay

                    that trumpets loudly
                    down suburban lanes

It does not sit drunken
upon the twilight bench

                    knowing feeble hands
                    make a world lame

Neither does my anger
bellow inaudible

                    into a deaf swollen ear
                    that eyes
                        droppings
                        yellow piss
                        caking
                        the sick
                        brick
                        wall.

A cacophony
disposed and destitute
dreams
unnurtured
crumpled

They are swollen bellies
with the lard of poverty

> quick fill of burgers
> hot dogs and drenched
> crazy salads (no horn of plenty here!)
> mall food.

This retrospect explosion
of nightmare syncopation

> adds subtlety to the scream
> that carries down the ear
> of a deaf suburb.

SCAPING THE LAND

The grass cut
lies brown
and dead dry.
In black garbage bags
its weight exceeds
the strength of hands

With me
it shall
stay
for a while.

SOIL OF EXCESS (TABLA POEM)

P[bh]ale—S[h]il-v[ah]—D[h]ay
>back drops (tirkat dhin)
>against (te dha tin)
>dark fol/[dha]/iage/[gedhindhin]
>of our exis[dha]tence.

T[e]ree—T[e][hu]runks—Stand[h]
>Taal aw/ay /fro/m
>Consonance per/fect ang/les
>al/w/[h]ays
>they lean towards
>a spring
>of life.

L[h]imp—L[h]eaf—Bran/[h]ches
>hanging
>the dying hands
>drawn
>to soil
>return
>rebirth.

Tirkat dhin dha Tirkat dha dhin
Tirkat dhin gha Tirkat gha dhin

yet this . . .
>the mere
>drunken cycle
>dhathicathin/dhathicadhin/dha
>of hardship

this an inebriate eye
upon
drunken earth
glancing—
dhathicathin/dhathicadhin/dha

This—a mouth that gurgles
            speaks as the soil
            that flows with excess
            (finish with Dadra Taal Improvisation
            te dha dhage dhin taghadhindha dhin)

REDEMPTION

So the sun shines
So the clouds
sit tranquil
ready to redeem
the black sheep
lost
in a desert of drifting
memory.

Redemption
works a one way street
She is a sultry singer
of a cool cool breeze
singing:

oh father of my child
so soon you shun me
how quick
you begin the walk
to find a new pair
of raggedy shoes.

Redemption
works my street
her lips stand full red
her broken nets
have let
all the fish escape.

But when I lay
my black head
against her
pale bosom
the clouds speak
no more to me.

            upstairs
            the sun shines
            on a few
            virgin fields

            but in my heart
            the sun shines
            on her soul.

and now
the clouds
speak
no more
to me.

LOVE MARRIAGE

As the priest abstains
the air rings out silent blessings

As my congregation falters
the breeze secures our love
showers our path with sweet petals

From indigo sky falls 'puteh'
from the rose, lilac and carnation
in cream crimson and blue we shimmer

Stems invisible arc the one sky
feeling injustice we
of engendered swollen pain
the heart of a segregated love
seek out union with each other's difference

Yet
my open palm
catching clenching
petals knuckles tighten
liquid forms around crushed velvet
aroma air absorbs skin
and one hand envelopes another

So when your lips touch velvet
   and drink from my fountains
   'Puteh de paani'
   my hand takes
   in your blood 'lovesoul'

Deep in the one sky
   nebulous blue utterance
   multiplies into the rapture of Parvati
   the petal fingers striking the one drum
   petal sounds stringing melody

And now my heart you
   my love the sky the eternal shrouds
   of heaven intertwine
   as vines and stems
   to create unconscious raw silhouettes
   of music as silent ether
   consecrates our love.

PAUPER IN THE CLASSROOM, OR
STUDENT UNDERGRAD(UAL) LITERARY HYPNOSIS

We are not robust

                are we?

lending ourselves
to circles of thought

                (desperate proliferation)

extending ourselves
to banal visionaries
        who throw
        convolution
        into our ears

            and we hear!

        lost melodies
        that we almost create
        undermined
        by the footnote
        that tells all from where
        we thought

as we have no
        con/text

asking the Crackling Cowboy
            to crackle some soul
            into our ears of lead
                        - sprinkle some of your seed please -

asking the bellowing bear
with a tongue of honey
            to extend her hand
while she blasts
our thoughts into
                oblivion
melodizing her own
textual/con/job

            tuning us into her
            frequency:

                        LITERARY TRADITION IS

                        OURS AS MUSE

                        WE CONGEAL AROUND IT

                        LIKE

                        GLAZE ON A HAM

Ourselves
obtuse, oblique
like a dying
glow worm
worming into darkness

syncopating verbiage
into natural incoherence
the discordant tune

'and when day
into sonorous
fog
breaks'

We like
shuffling mutts
move toward
the left-overs
Now
smelling
a creeping scent
we force ourselves
chewing, crunching, grinding
on rancid

-bones-

that give us
half words
half meaning
partial language.

Though still
lizard creaks
with smile
pours dust on our heads
and tells us
                    - look out for this image
                    it means death -

So we look for it
in all corners
in the space between
the line of the word
the line of meaning

and then the door
opens
with the robust scholar
pointing
a monolithic finger
(for emphasis)
                    at one of us
                    and brings us in

And We Go!

THE ANSWER TO MIDNIGHT

To make the world witness
to a struggle that occurs
in the distant horizon
of one's eye.

> the design
> is beautiful (no!)
> rainbows
> of segregated colours
> defying law of latitude
> creating space
> for social order
> demanding
> acknowledgement
> for existing hierarchy.

> 'some where o'er this rainbow
> a constitution unwritten'

To footnote history
the story of man
        literature
NO!
story of struggle
story of knowing
not
where his story began
whose story?   The Imperialist's story
          The story of the new order
          The birth of midnight

The martyr of our soil
The story of our faith
    or
the story of me

and
to whom do I footnote?

                    'stand upon the isthmus'

declare yourself—claim yourself:

                    'I have nothing to claim
                        except my genius'

voice within the vacuum
that says:
        my flag is a ragged cloth
        the stain of dried blood
        the relic of independence
        the wheel hardly forms a centre
        colours stand muted and bare
        now the story is of _____!

So now I know
I shall not crack
my finger bones
before I begin:

a trail
a stoic course
feet touch earth
a summer vale
yet
here
the terrible sun
the shadow forest
existence in the cave
the still negative
the inverted
photograph.

where
hot voice breathes
upon suffering shoulders.

DEPRIVATION

Deprivation
        in this isolation
        chamber

Composing reality
        one day I
        mad with hunger
        cannot talk
        of nectar and Elysium

My soul
        burns for fire
        in a hot wave
        today the destroyer
        is within me.

THE 4 O'CLOCK POEM

The waves of wind
that rustle leaves
in trees drowned
by the floodlight
against the green.

> the folly of muse-ic
> the scratching
> that goes on
> while the earth
> lays in snoring
> slumber
> (A story is being made)

The cat of scratches
lengthens its back
and digs its claws
into a pale green
of a sleepless house coat
upon a sleepless soul

> the fall in night
> awakens one
> to a dreary time
> the searcher meets
> chaos.

The cross of legs
done by a man
whose body numb
cracks as the horrid
ticking lays down
torture for his moment.

the place of rest
is home to emptiness
to sacrifice a sentient love
is a particular death.

THE CRADLE SEEN

Quite breathing
a crib with
baby bears scattered
around
the one who sleeps

She calls them
to lay down
their heads
and join her
in sleep

Natasha
becoming mother
before
ceasing
to be
my baby child

IMPROVISATIONS UPON DEMOCRACY: PART ONE (MARRIAGE ON EARTH)

I stand cultivated
nurturing myself
shaping and moulding
within this
hetero-sexual-genius-world

       one man, one vote
       democratic truth
       right!

       to such truths
       we sold ourselves
       narrowing our minds
       into a reality
       of dogma

'take it home'
I say.

       He sat upon the chair
       nibbling of the food
       staring idly out the window
       while on his left
       She sat upon the chair
       looking
       into the brown gravy

Both voted for this
Both agreed to the other

Letting down her hair
at night
She wished for a ferocious
storm
a real howler
musing on Heathcliff
she dreamed of a dark lover
As
He in his pudging
farting wheezing body
fell upon her as he
always did
- from head to toe -

She whispered
here be the beauty
of our bond

Humping, Slapping
Democracy
one married thigh
rubbing equally
against
the other

Both
already lost within
night orgies of fantasy
and he drowned in blond
pussy
both rich with the sweat
and juice of anonymous
pulsating flesh.

IMPROVISATIONS UPON DEMOCRACY : PART TWO (MARRIAGE IN MYTHOS)

To begin
there are shadows
in my eyes
thatched roofs collapsing
walls crumbling
slowly
line around my landscape
                    - The King -
                    - The King Lays Dying -

She told him
as he polished his throne
you do not love me
you do not please me
you lack the knowledge
of my desires
you lack the wisdom
of my insights

Strangling within her
death hold
dry seeded
he carried on
polishing slower now

Again
the crevices
of my soul
reach toward
my mother rock

To be real
he had built
home
in seven years
she created the succour
within

Kneeling knight
that he is
asked: Oh, Beloved
         How shall I make
         myself worthy
         of your love?

(with a baby on her hip
  she received him officiously)

         It was the clock
         that struck
         him out of her
         maternity (for maternity is all she had)

Finality is not
good enough for
desperate kings
and knights looking
for validation

Love then speaks: man (kings and knights included)
I live within your heart
primacy is my real name
yet you call me democracy
and embody me with
a scale and a blindfold

Maternity, Paternity, Fraternity
brotherhood and sisterhood
are the false avatars you placed
in my name, I was here before
your mind ate that bad fruit
before Shiva danced divinity
at his love's request

I am your Conundrum
I am the paradox
of your depraved piety

I am no woman
I am no man
I am no mother
I am no father

try to be worthy
of me
you shall find yourself
deserted
think me as divine
I shall make you
wretched as the night
that comes in the day
neither am I of night
nor of the day
in such binaries
you cannot comprehend
my totality that lives
within your heart

I speak without voice
without position
with these words of disunity
Only then will you
know yourself and
the chaos of your affliction.

REFLECTION

Eye catches
shadow eye
in contemplation

Beyond
a slumbering world
slate melts
into grey

A figure
looking
upon the road
making sure that
death did not die
that
the 134 is on time
and
ticking

Behind
curtains
the perpetual hum
of false shadows
play on the
wall

Outside
drains the rainpipe
drones to persist
leads

the shadow soul
through
waking sleep
into a fixed place
connected
by movement

Distant traffic roars
howls and shrieks
the crumbling
of a world
begins

Solid becomes liquid
Line disperses into
movement

insubordinate . . .

chaos . . .

yet
face invades
ivory skull sees
the eye protrudes
quick and
jumps
again

and asks:
> Have you found it yet?

Silent are
eyes that
answer.

TO A FRIEND ON A COAST LINE

Do we stand upon this quiet reef?
We look towards the ocean line
Our gaze follows the reflecting wave
fresh blood shining upon aquatic stage
I see the dove and crane fly
the crane swoops to the water
and with a savage circle
moves in on its prey

We stand upon this isthmus?
We look to the gulls howling
into the wind
the wings shadow
our minds
the issue recedes quickly
into oblivion
I turn to you with dry
crackling eyes

You turn to gaze once more
at the ocean line

Do we stand upon this quite
consoling reef?

NUTTY AND NAKED

Glass melted in droplets from heaven
mirrors reflecting a dull translucence
cold to touch, but soon the body warms
damp, yet steaming, the body warms
dribbles of divinity, like catch-all phrases
they speak without doubt, pure conviction
If you hold out your hands, you catch them
they follow down your lines like a known road
explaining to you the past the present the future

I wonder if all poets hold out their hands
I wonder if poets believe these small deities

If I walk out naked in this metallic grey
and absorb these drops into my open skin
am I then a god? Then am I the real one
a channeller of the Great Spirit
or
am I walking nutty naked in the enfolding rain?

NOCTURNAL SONG

This nocturnal song
longing for melody
searching out essence
that cauterizes the soul

Soul utterance

        song of voice

         yet
         blind
           cataract eye
             transcribing for
             cadence

To form
a cave
pull in the eye
     the storm
     absent content
of angry love   fear
       lust   death

       Can one just say: Ah, my heart
       feels empty tonight—tonight my heart
       is swollen and heavy, tonight the wind
       cracks upon my eardrum—tonight
       I look for some
             thing

Here
a form
the dead balcony
where cackling laughter
gives a mountain
lascivious shapes
here
the peace is lame tonight

A querulous voice takes shape
and yet
              absence
                        anonymity
smothers this sound
this balcony
with a sordid viewscape
              (and did i create this world?)

              yes
              I shall not lay
              upon the ground
              that shapes me

              on air that
              fills my ears
              with the cacophony
              of the many

In looking
the eye drifts
ears vibrate
   and
when I limp towards
the phantom night
whose wraith
makes a mountain
look like a young
nubile form
   where
utterance is lost
a shape melts
and form diffuses
again
   then
the moment
allows me to lament
          shed tears
       and know
that I lost my sight
before I began
to see

QUEST   SHUN

Lament   of dead souls
and dance   and
sacrifice
a dried
leaf   love

I   have a
      dry leaf
      for you

              It crumples
              It falls

scatters across
desert fields

              It returns
      love

this leaf

      I have
        brought
           to you

A WALK THROUGH PURTAPURRA VILLAGE

On a walk in a past time
a [k]narled tree passes our way
here it is, he says
the tree I passed each day

i am now looking before me
beneath my feet, the roots feel
they search out long and hard
i dig deep into my father's eye.

unborn;

reborn.
On a day, my new father
takes my hand and joins
a hand joined to a hand
there; we are done
we are bound for eternity
she is younger, i cannot see her
she is a distant family
the match is fine.

A silence pervades
the breeze is gentle
the azure sky is loving
here, peace exists affirmed.

I step over a snaking root
that feels strong and heavy
like a far reaching memory
it too tries to feed on belonging.

A FAMILY FUNCTION

... the voice is in
our voice.
perspiring hopes
drip heavy in a dream
home is fertile
mind is my soil . . .

My father's hand
is a rough silence
he is the poetic
the serviceable server
our soul song sings
through his lips
his voice continues on

. . . the twilight brings
the last visit
to her husband
a celebration
before a dark death . . .

our soul flows
outside the sound
our eyes close
to this anguish
our drunken eyes
follow downwards
searching answers
deep in our past

. . . arriving with beauty
concealed
s/he
the first of our brave
the last of our lions . . .

now we are hanging
and maimed on the
conquering cross.

BIRTH?

From where the
d[h]an [te] lions g [h] row

I come out of a snagging soil
fresh, cool, and crooked.
(Tirkat, Dha, Tirdhadhin)

Hideous then
to be longing
this way
my mind straining upwards
towards Elysium
while a sonorous Rag Piloo
stretches me out
across the plain.
(Four Beat Cycle—Dhage Dhinta Dhage Dhinta)

I am the nurturer
of battling visions
shiva is poking out
of my soul.

Beauty:	Harmony in	te dha dhin
	cyclic rhythmic	te dha dhin
	motions of the universe	te dha dhin
	from my soul breath	te dha dhin
	to my dance of the galaxies	te dha dhin
	of the instinctual	te dha dhin
	existence.	te dha dhin

Bestial: In the smoking b[h]ar
          I have in between
          a joint
          a pint
          and cough up
          phlegm as thick
          and black as my night.

          Luridly, lasciviously
          I, open-mouthed
          couldn't give
          two stools about
          celestial music

F[h]resh, c[hu]ool and cr[h]ooke[i]d[ha]
I creep out of the snagging soil
where the d[h]an[te]lio[h]ns g[h]row.

GHAZAL'S BREATH (PUNJABI STYLE)

Carry oh carry me to the place
where lilacs fall from every space

Oh carry these petals below my love
Ah sanctuary love, secure our fate

So carry my heart upon open palms
rise up, break free from your nocturnal cage

Sing out, rejoice that upon rose bed soil
lay scented ovals whose blessings we take

So on our horizon sweet voices lace
these motions of you, I with eternal embrace.

CREATION (ELIOTESQUE)

Lend an ear
to my thought

I have cancelled
myself out

desperation is a game, knowing
where the start begins, ending
when the black night dies, tending
the flock of memories
within the twilight pasture.

I remember you
when I was young
then, you seemed
old.
now
I, a crackling preacher
bending the ways
I see your twisted path
feeling ancient.

In your youth
the night fantastic
wild with uncertainty
steaming
glass

we would peer out
to see if the
mad boy
stood naked at
his sill.

lend me your ear
night music plays
within silence
clanging dissonance
surrounding us.

Sleepless I travel, watching
the autumn leaf rot, knowing
the bronze flaked path, leading
to my insomniac soil, bearing
the carcasses of the seasons.

distance
resembles
the sound
of silence

A heavy night
carrying lead down
upon my shoulders.

And you lying
letting
twilight resonate
your soft belly form
nurturing your womb
and resting
within one purity
alas
I look to you
see how the moon
that sheds sight
within mine eyes
can see the cosmos
unfold
within your hour.

ANDROGYNY ONE

How would you like me
tonight?

Am I to be Heathcliff?
Am I to be Hamlet?
Am I to be Prufrock?

How would you then
like me
to be?

Answer carefully
        slowly

lest the words fall
down
this
funnel of a voice
Beware!
for they might
merge with
Belinda and Moll

and then
we will have problems.

ANDROGYNY TWO: THE WOMB/MAN

sultry s/he
slithered over
silk sand
looking to
explode into
someone's skin.

silky s/he strode.

Froth washed
over soft flesh
flexing small
taut muscles
sinewy shadows
perplexed limbs
filling with venom
s/he lay
motionless
as s/he
danced out
into the
sea.

ANDROGYNY THREE: FAITH

A withered tree
swayed
near a dry well.
s/he
looked at the
worm eating at
the bark
s/he burned
acidic eyes
into the skin.

Into the well
s/he looked
finding brittle pools
of dust
at the dark end
of a bruised
tunnel.

To replenish
the flow
s/he opened
up the zipper
took out her hood
and
pissed into
the well.

The spring
was replenished
the tree
was
ressur/erected.

S / HE

There is a paleness
in my sky
clouding ennui
over my shoulders

This day last week
a world suspends
a fraction of no
second, but a fracture
of emotions

Lost into earth
diffused into dandy/lions
deciduous forests shedding
life
lived on
fertile fields
now decomposed
now returned, the
leaf crumbles into
oblivion

And in this fractured skull
mind follows diurnal course.
ah, this disassociation
knowing the death of this land
is the death of the poet's soul

fraction 1: you take this for granted
             that a man must eat and give
             a child must be clothed
             and fed
             A woman must feel
             the loving arms of
             [his] stability

fraction 2: what you did not know
             that s/he the child
             that struggled into the
             heart of the maple leaf
             was a great sacrifice

             that s/he the child
             in the eye of
             "Nanak's follower"
             was born in England
             nurtured in the cold
             heart of a prairie land
             within impoverished sanctuary
             with permafrost caking
             and hardening the wheat fields

             That s/he the child
             brought to the carnivorous
             forest
             was burned into bitterness
             scorched into anger
             and broiled in humiliation

now

s/he the child
leaps up to apply
the last venomous strike
towards a multi-foliated enemy

s/he the child (?)
    the destroyer (?)
    the giver (?)
    the nurturer (?)
of life (?)
strikes out
the sounds of gritting soul:

      Dha Dhin
      Dha Dhin Dhin
      ThicaThicaThum
      Te Dhi . . . Dhi Dhin Dhum
      Ta Dhi . . . Dhi
      ThicaThicaThicaTa Thum
      Dhin.

RE/COGNIZE

Re-cognize
    clarity
    crisp water falling
    crashing into foam

    cognize
    beauty
    anorexic
    model
    modelling a lifestyle
    cognize
    aesthetic
    multi foliate
    rose petal lush
    and young.

    cognize
    movement
    sun, moon, flower
    grass, earth, mountain
        —mother earth mountain
        —sister flower song
        —Diana's bright tonight
        —"Shall I compare thee
          to the sun."

cognize
faith
healing the lame
giving to the poor
loving the impoverished
Pitying the impure.

Re-cognize
our
past.

VANCOUVER: BHARAT MATHA REMOVED

Again
the night turns
inside out

    angry passion
    bottled up
    pouring out of hollows
    in my skin

Throat
parching upon infinity
crackles and heaves
into a tense silence

        (is there noise in the air I cough on?)

A number of things:
        ticking like the 4-beat rhythm
        in my mind yet
        my heart missing on one tic
        doubling up on the toc:
        ThicaThicaThica . . . Thica
        Dhum . Dhin
        ThicaThicaThica.

        Uhmmm, Uhmmmm, AUhmmmmmmm. . . .

no celestial music
no
only the undying
voice of the microwave and fridge
AUHMMMMMMMMMMMMMMMMMMMMMMM.

Looking in
a reflecting window
a window looking
within

> I see cracks upon my lips
> stubborn stubble caking
> my holy clay face.

Yes
this is 'I'
this cliché
cartoon
with eyes bulging
bags sunken
a groin alive and dead
on one spot
an insomnia night
howling into this abyss
that is my soul.

> Affirmation #1: I am the abyss, the abysmal
> descent is inside
> self actualization is inside
> you are not what you eat

you are what you have eaten
I have eaten someone's
rotten fruit, the fruit
sits still in my stomach
my stomach descends

time to move on.

Am I terse yet?

My machinery is my poetry
it runs smoothly when well greased
full of hot fuel and always maintained

this is the lesson.

My eye never moves away from the machine
my mind is always on the passing streets
the industrial death yards
we call the centre for our commerce.

When I see
the snowcaps of Grouse
Seymour and Whistler
I become numb inside
because I know a different person
lives those dreams
        'they always smile when they ski'

you see
today
we cannot talk
of the undulating landscapes
of the roman[tics]
those luxuriant aesthetics
are not for us.

No

My lesson is hard
and brittle
it's Miller time
without the beer and testes
because I am no great man
and I have no great balls
and this life is no great tragedy.

time to move on.

When I look out
over English Bay
      or
      "Wretch" Beach
I see tankers
      and pleasure boats
      exchanging friendly
      manoeuvres
            'they always smile when they
            ride those waves'

And when I reach into the
       pine rich trails
       of Golden Ears Park
       and set foot upon
       Allouette Beach with
       my family, food, and gin
              'I know a whole culture smiles
              vacuously at me and past me'

And in my solitude
in one moment
my eye looks
to the vegetation
of my home soil
I heave as mother rock
heaves
I cough once more

An orange smoke
that reels me
back into the plight
the home within
       the forest
       the city
keeping out the rhythm
our urbanity smoothes away
the cycles that are in my bones
the seasons of the farmer

Stasis our illusion
Stasis our control
without this is

Thicathic Dhum DhinDhum
Thica Dhica Dhum Dhin
Dhica Thica Thum.

PISSING POEM

I'm pissing and wishing
wishing for a pissing
I'm sipping and pissing
the day
I'm wishing
wishing for the piss
pissing for one wish
one wish
to fly myself
away.

THE GOOD LIFE

You live in a good-looking
tarnished tenement
with fluctuating rent patterns
due to fluctuating income
with cupboards
half-empty, or half-full.

The job you work at
is essentially essential
staticity directing transience
you are a parking lot attendant.

Not quite so poor
you can buy big coffees
but you cannot afford
your self worth.

ON MY WRITING

Let us say then
I am wrong
Let us then say
I have no Depth

.

Integrity

.

Clarity

.

And yet
I have invaded you
I make you
re/cognize
behind the words

Then let us say
I have one advantage
I am the muse's whore
tired, used, and wise.

HOW TO WALK

Keep one 'I' closed
one eye open

feel the roaming
carry heavy upon
your brow—the blind insight

Passing through the doors
on the way out
merge into anonymity
forget your 'I'
but keep the other eye open.

LOVE

T[dh]ime
for/
[dhumte]ever[-dhatin]
parts us

today jagged snow flake
erects
cold p[bh]alace
The day crimson
and[h] cold[h] the t[dh]ime
burning and cold the air
hot and cold

T[h]e soul t[dh]ough
warms in passion
silent hands burn
cold touch

Lips flaming raw
Yet smooth touch
I come to you
in a flow of mel[dhi]ng snow
and[h]
through our baby's smile

KISMET (THE POET'S PATH)

The hand lies heavy
the eye droops
dismayed
Failure   the failed cycle
bitter memory livid
rage   hunger
the hunger artist

The spell, pulsating mind
I am
inept? clumsy? distracted?
my burnt offerings
the world
of hand to eye
co-ordination
the world
of monetary mobility

this world of statutory holidays

MOMENTARY DEPARTURE

I asked my soul
to leave
through the crack
of the moulding curtain
that showed me
the onset of
luminous dawn

I reached up
into the bristling branches
only to turn
and look
through the crack
of my curtain
to see my beloved struggling
with our child
caressing and cursing
and then I asked my soul
to rejoin
once more
the occurring world.

THE REFRAIN

Because
I know
that you
love me
but fall short
of knowing
who I am

I then
choose to
come to you
as the mirror
of your love,
then you shall
see me
as you are
within your love
and you will
know
I am the loved
loving on the
outside.

THE BOOTH

Enter the booth
and become invisible

On the street
I wear a Michelangelo
tie
and my navy blue
pants
flap in the breeze

these are my modern vestiges

Enter the booth
and become invisible
I know like always
I know
i become
part of the parking
machinery: Amano time clock
                syscorp cash register
                credit card machine
                automated ticket dispensers
                and a nice smiling immigrant
                with a guttural accent
                Punjabi, Ismaili, Chinese,
                Tamil, or Ethiopian
                a reserve labour pool
                of poor Bengalis
                Somalians and Fijians

with a few
bohemian anglophiles

I know
I always know
how to be part
of this machinery.

CUSTOMER SERVICE

We do accept
MasterCard, Visa
and American Express

And this booth
also accepts
nickels, dimes
or a quarter of
your time

For this tip
of a dime
buys me time
on the bus
or adds to my
swelling change purse
though
my wallet bare
except for the
bills of bills
that
forestalls
my equality
flattens out
my marketability
leaving me
to wake up
to another
parking booth day.

I WORK ON YOUR HOLY DAYS

when you are
here for new year's eve
or the annual christmas party
or come down to the city
on a family outing
I am here to tend
to your happiness.
Though I am being paid
double time today
I am here frozen
with smile, with an
emptiness in my heart
without the warm face
of my beloved
or the love of my babe
who knows that 'daddysatwork'

FRAGMENTS

again
yet this day
gains me enough
time this month
time enough
to break even

Here
in my booth
we get along well
the punjabi trusts
the ismaili as much
as the chinese
trusts
either

I Am Impow-Tent
I Am Potent
With Impow-Tense
I Am
I Am Tense
With A Sense
Of Impow-Tence
I Am
Impow-Tense I Am
am i tense in this booth?
my booth is impo-tant.

I Am
I Am Impow-Tent & Tense
In my Impow-Tense
I am
I NKOW.

THE EXCHANGE

In the booth
things become symbolic

Bits and pieces
of conversation
like a bullshitter
shitting on you
about how easy
it is to get laid
these days
while you feel
inadequate and ugly
as the cellular
keeps on talking
as the boss
throws you the money
and complains
about the price of parking
while sitting in a souped-up Saab
Oh! Sahib.

And your smile
common courtesy
and service
bears no relevance
except in the validation
of validating the ticket

continuing to hand out
freedom and open access
while being wired up
within four panes
of security glass.

SLIVER IN THOUGHT

A sliver in thought

A tranquil place of love
rupturing into a 4:30 morning
another day of boredom
noxious car fumes that worsen
when using high grade fuel
to suffocate your soul.

THE SOOTHSAYER'S WORDS

In my youth
I was told by
the local soothsayer
visiting Purtappra

'Bhindar, you will wield great power
to move, to change yourself, to be
chameleon to your earth, you will
Bhindar, move, direct people, Bhindar,
you will sit in a still centre and
surrounding you will be a transient mass'

Now,
ten years later
a Canadian in the place
of an Indian
Having now made
Vancouver my home
while Purtappra lays
secluded in memories
I stand in my booth
wielding the spirit
to direct traffic
to be the lot attendant
to a transient mass
of cellular talking
smoothies
whom I must gently
attend to and respect

And now
I know a soothsayer's words
are always laced
with the power
of subtleties
the impotence of impact
the trick of the trickster
sugaring the ego.

THE MONTHLIES

The one who owns
the fur shop
drives in and out
of the lot
without acknowledging
me though
such a straight face
is telling of a past
atomic interned humiliation
His grey suit and turtleneck
keep him stoned
to the centre view

The taxi business owner
knows the struggle
and smiles the assurance
of success
and greets me
with genuine optimism
His teeth of ivory shine
and his secretary keeps his day planner booked

The owner of the Oriental store
is also one who knows
but he loves his
position he is genuine
in quick hellos and
quick goodbyes

The beautiful blonde
hotel manager
knows how far she
has come
and how hard
she has worked
and will of course say
hello and goodbye
with the ease of her beauty
it leads her onwards

The old man
in the V-8 Burgundy
is quiet and gruff
and always nods.
He's a red-throbbing-nose regular
and knows how to take care of himself

The jeweller and his wife
are elegant Europeans
They are also Canadians
which allows them
humanity enough
to condescend to such
acknowledgements   -it is written in our constitution-
their daughter believes
this is my career

and whenever my
two loves visit me
at my booth
she colloquially asks
'training the family
  are you'

THE PARAMETERS WITHIN

1.

You cannot work here
as maintenance for
fourteen dollars an hour
as a summer job
No
We want you
to commit to full time
degradation
We only allow
white students
to cut our
municipal
grasses
every year.

2.

Parking lot attendants
are not supposed to have
chips on their shoulders

I say: better to have a chip
          rather than no shoulder
          at all.

3.
The old man came by
'first night' in full swing
looked at me
with a smile
I knew there were
diamonds in his eyes

He passed by the booth
looked at me again
pulled out his
complimentary 'first night' badge
handed it to me
and with a well-wishing
wink of the eye
said 'here, enjoy the night'
smiling back
I asked him if he would
invite me
to one of his
tuxedo-medallion-family-balls.

ME AND HER C-SECTION

To place my forehead
against your hand
pleading for nothing
feeling the knot
in my soul tighten
my face burns
my throat parched
as I look into your
sad face
as they bore into you

To look up
over their green
curtain
look toward your
battle incision
your war scar
your suffering
and ripples of pain
to caress your arm
as four hands
pull out
life from your womb
and silently pray
a ritual
hoping
for your eyes to shine
to love you again
as I loved you
before.

Kiss
for open palm
life line
against my lips.

THE DELIVERY

Your skin pale
fluorescence
within a tired light

Your arms heavy
eyes closed
and breath quiet

Shards of crystal inhaled
the anaesthetic mask
count the numbers: 1 2 3 4 5 6 7 . . .

My struggle
to keep myself
from moaning
from saying 'sorry'
as your pain
ensnares my love
to stop the tears
within my eyes
lest a roomful
of physicians guide
me outside to compose
my pain on a cold steel stool

To stop my anguish
at the sacrifice
you made for me
as I hold
on to your arm
for my life,
never letting you relinquish
the burden of your care
even as your eyes flutter
through a desiccating sleep

To hold onto the ritual
of prayer, and pray for
my deliverance
from these knots within
and see our love resonate
again on the face
of our child.

PIECING IT TOGETHER

To gather myself
up again

Piece each brittle
fragment so

I can become
whole

To gather these
bits of debris
as they fall
out of me

to string the moment

This is how
I face the world
renewed

As my old youth
dies young.

GOING HOME

I am at my loneliest
when I leave the booth.

When I cross over
to cut through the
art gallery green
making my way
to the Granville bus stop
I am befriended by the night.

With each step taken
my soul burns
the darkness assures my absence
I am shade creeping
along the crevices
a transposed life
appearing and disappearing.

My appearance is worn
my clothes disordered
by the movement in my booth.

And then I catch
the #14 Hastings
and watch the bustling aunties
who have just finished
their midnight shifts
and are on their way home.

I watch their laughing faces
as they tell their stories
of ridiculous customers and
who is coming who is going and
who is marrying and why the boss
won't give them the day shift.

I catch the #14 Hastings
watching mirrors
of myself
in all these faces
acting out
the same
deprivation.

BITTERNESS: IN TEEN TAAL
(SIXTEEN-BEAT RHYTHM CYCLE)

is seeing the bags under your eyes swell
while working ten straight days
at eight twenty-six an hour
or[-dha]

it is sitting in a small visible booth
knowing that being turned down equality and
    enfranchisement
has left you invisible and poor
or[-dha]

it is the transience of going from one shift to the next
to the next lot to another lot bewildering your spirit
sapping the strength from your soul
draining the will to fight and continue
or[-dha]

it is waking up at four in the morning dreaming
that you went mad at work and wandered the city
with strangers gawking at you but not seeing you
while you wandered knowing not where your home is
where your family has gone or where you came from
and losing yourself to raving insanity
or[-dha]

it is the falling
the fathomless fall into remembering what should have been
when you called yourself a student of literature
while slashing your/self as a lot attendant
and how you were supposed to begin
at thirty thousand a year
or[-dha]

the smile you remember as you loved your beloved
more than anything else this world allowed you
on your marriage day and how you were cast out
onto an unknown sea, as the island of your love
drifted away quietly, fertilizing as she disappeared
or[-dha]

knowing that when the question is called about racism
social justice, socialism, communism, and marxism
it is always you who is the resident expert on these issues
or[-dha]

the raving of your soul as your mind unravels and you
don't know how to stop it, the noise in your brain
the hurt in your eyes, the explosion in your heart
when you must choose between an exhausted
    impoverished
Egalitarian home life, or a disconnected blow job
and an indifferent night of sex
or[-dha]

looking to see how equality between men and women
has a better chance at success
when both individuals make fifty thousand-plus a year
and the question of domestic duties
is solved by a Phillipino nanny hired at five-fifty an hour
or[-dha]

the chain of delegated events as the company operations
    manager
orders the district supervisor to clean a B&E vehicle up
who then orders the lot manager to clean the mess
while temporarily becoming lot manager, and the lot manager
orders you to go clean the mess up as the lot manager enters
your visible booth momentarily to become invisible, and
you saunter up to clean the mess of a B&E vehicle
as the owner supervises the work effort and looks over you
but never at you
or[-dha]

the virulent insults levelled at you by a civil individual
who turns foul-mouthed when asked to pay for parking
and the only thing the customer can say is
fuck this and fuck that and fuck you
as he drives away in his souped-up mercedes
or[-dha]

the helplesness you feel yourself moving away from your lover,
family get-togethers and knowing how much your child misses
you when you are at work in the evenings and on the weekends
and how much you lose for every hour you have gained eight
twenty-six and the choice between the welfare line, humiliation,
and failure in your family's eyes and the endless journey in a
dark fluorescence
sitting in the booth with a disconnected family
who doesn't know you
seem like the impossible nightmare
that should never have happened
has happened to you
and has condemned you
to this existence.

bitterness burning out my soul.

FACES OF RECOGNITION

My sun is a gol[dhin] wom[bh]an
My sky is an azure ma[h]n
My cloud is a milk[hy] [gh]irl
My mist is a see through [bh]oy.

The tree is my [bh]rown matta
The soil is my [dha]rk fa[dhe]r
The wheat[dh] is my floured bro[dhe]r
The corn is my gold yellow sis[dhe]r (gha/dhi/dhum/dhage)

The thorn and rose are my beloved
And I am the opening womb

This poem I give birth to
Is my rose child of a thousand tears
dropping out a roopak taal.

A BIRTH DAY SONG

The day is of rejoice
    two years before
    when I became 'daddy'
    born into my life
    through
    my love's
    rupturing womb
    she came.

Now
she a sleeping sight
not two minutes before
crying against weariness
she has lain down
calling on her stuffed children
to join her ceremony
and close the eye
on their infancy
        and open anew
        to the other side
        where everything
        is animated.

There is a quiet
in my soul
    no quiet content
but
the quiet sacrifice
we gave ourselves to
self-immolation

made less burning
more smouldering
by the joy of
her love.

It is nearing
another end.
The cycle
The branches outside
her window sill
are bare
the grey silt hangs
loosely upon our
earth.

And yet
hot are
my tears

Hot is
my love

Hot are
the hands
pressing quietly
against her
rosen cheek.

This moment
pierces deep
deep inside
brings forth
absolution?

Today
I am happy
to go further
towards an end.

A FLOWERY DRESS

[Bh]len[dhin]g in[thu] you
I catch sight
of a car/nivo/rous worl[dh].

Your eyes
I see relinquishing
reality composed
of dogma.

What it brings
this revolution
is a fall
into the abyss.

You see
eyes
you cannot have
lips
you cannot kiss
warmth
you cannot feel.

Now coming apart
I know
from where
in your black soul
you decided to buy
a flowery dress.

THE COLLISION

You remind me of
far back before my birth.
Ah yes, it is that fair skin
those sandy blonde locks
and opulent emeralds you carry for eyes.

You remind me of Ganga
when it drifted sea green
past my eyes as I was carried
by our North Sea gas-converted camper
and my eyes changed a slight shade forever.

Your translucent smile is a remnant
of old tastes mingled with passion
yearnings to transgress forth
your owned views, cross the line of decorum
Parvati to my passion, nurturer to my extremes
lover seeping out of my senses.

The Victorian forehead
stands ready for the eternal question
ready to defeat
a dying myth
to rip out the four ventricles of my soul
while kissing my left nipple and holding me together
you are my conundrum.

There is purity too
and innocence written
in you and on you
the aristocratic façade
you have grown to love
as Forester's Malabar Coast
quietly palpitates into your
ongoing creation.

I, the sadhu
who melted into the dark
who dissipated into the caves
and shadows
yearned for you more than
my Bengali master.

Poverty is beauty to your senses.

A raw anger is sensual for you
you are an ivory statue
sentient yet dead trying to live through
rum, gin, and vodka
you dance with an anonymity
allowing you the abandonment
of a black dance floor.
A much needed attention
that gives you life.

You will always live in public
You will always want to own this space.

SOUL DROWNING

A Culminating Present

scraps for stories
ragged cloth holding
a brow's sweat,
absorbing daily
memories.

Shafts of Light
encroaching onto an already blazing day.

> \- But it was our sun then and these stories we
> held close to the heart and told in whispers
> and silences, when everyone outside looked
> the other way
> stories for today -

Amidst
scattered stories
of eminent orgies
in violence and curfews
keeping toward the cold corner
of each transmission
-POLICE STATE BATTLES VISIONS-
within itself to the outside.

I saw Vishnu lurking
in the background breathing a karmatic sigh
I felt whispers of Allah quietly
probing the depth of the mob's soul
I heard Nanak looking to settle

an absent argument gone mad—as our house contorted to
                a single sign of the five Ks
                and we became lost in the
                well of the word.

I knew my flesh crawled
along streets and took flight
in words of a not so paupered
pauper
wearing
cotton as an emblem
out of one ear, shuffling like
there was a truth about non-violence
that one's birth
or to whom one was born
did not matter.

Took flight again
hoping it would bring oblivion.

Falling from secular sky
I had thorns, blackberry trees, bushes
and a hunk of dogwood and cedar
enshrouding me in quiet, dizzying me
in lumber laughs
bristling forests
in my presence.

I can still hear it
the voices of transmigration
the sigh after partition
unnatural still sighs
four generations down the line.
Now it is the nerves that compete:

> "Bhindar, please cut out the excess,
> don't editorialize, don't go there,
> just phone for all the information,
> more easier that way, less money then,
> But make sure to keep the vision for
> Mr. Shumla, he is a respected client,
> give him a good write up, you know a good
> standing, after all Bhindar, Shumla and
> me, we're old friends, back there we were
> working on our dreams, Bhindar, you get
> my point.
> If you ask me Shumla has it right
> Punjab is for Punjabis, that's the
> difference."

(Oh, but what about Canada)

It was still there
Canada and the moan.
Carrying it with me.
The Variables:
a punjab
a sexist pig
an asshole

an idiot
and always belligerent.

And the sound
always there.
(as my heart
always hear, and here, not
their.)
Of riding in summer
as the stench of fields
repulsed
and the whispering grass
making uneasy waves
the lazy buttercup lime green
cutting through my brown feet
lifting my beloved cup
up to radiate the sun on
my shaded face.

Pitt River in its murky sheath
reflecting shards of the farmer
exiled out of the self.
Mali my torchlight, given
to me by birth
I, the gardener
nurture and grow
and protect
keep the garden
the flowers my children
my life with me in my poverty.

The Mali of a cleared-out section
memories of trees
a shine in my heart
the golden corn flower
and green leaves
I am prosaic now.

THE WORD

A word called word
worded up a meaning
And I meant to say
but
Can I then not
unword the word
unplant the meaning
turn the word inside
out
and
convince you what was
always inside but
never seen, or scened
or what the word
meant when it ebbed out
into the sea.

BRITISH BIRTH

I was born in
a white-coloured city
that had black railings
guarding over Edwardian
structures that set sail
down streets paved
with parks full of carnations
and roses, oh, Memorial Park
I hope you remember me.

But I wasn't born there.

Come into being
was a tenement on the east side
of the west.
A patch work
mouldy dreams that
crashed in mid-flight.

But I wasn't born there.
Dribbling streams
cascading rivers like an
immigrant looking for menial work.

Our Jamaican brothers
led the way to the dole house
and I
cared about nothing but chocolate
and mama's hand
softened by flowery moisturizer.

I began in a neighbourhood
of irish catholics, punjabi hindus, sikhs
and parsis.
Botner Road,
Unlike Blundell,
gave me blessings in gullies
full of nocturnal fears.

Blundell dressed me in self-loathing
as my poverty squealed in
my night through the fluttering
cupboards and the light
patter on the sour carpet.

Blundell
held me fixed to the core
bumming lunch money
from a friend that I
never repaid
and the quiet days
of crazy like berry bushes
in the backyard
only spoke of silences
while I knew jam
was waiting to come out of them.
I knew then

Blundell taught me.
The long faces
and cheap Christmases

- not like we celebrated anyway -
but I saw myself growing
out of my midnight lookout
street as I counted
the ways the shadows crept
over our muddied entrance.

Blundell was brutal
limbs filling out
clothing that stuck to
one's skin
and cheap shirts
papa bringing off-bacon
and a loaf of mouldy old bread
and mama breaking under the strain
looking to go mental
with anguish.

Blundell exchanged
A self
A Pitt Meadows self
A meadow full of pits
pulling down
into the psyche
hallway voices
whispering Punjabs and Pakis
Iron Maiden blasting out
through trigger-happy walls.

Pitt Meadows—a fixture
fixing to be big
but without big city attitude
come settle down here
we make any citizen welcome
though the annual blueberry festival
only showed Dutch and German farmers
working the berry fields.

Our fruit gone wild
with beer and piss
all over the green
Pitt Meadows Day
drove everyone wild
with a smile for Canada.

WHAT TO BE TOLD

Now [dha]
[dhu]what   shall[ta]
my-[thum]-soul-[thin]-say?

What [tirkat]
can I have
or[dha]   am allowed?

A pitcher full of water
[te]leak-ing[dhin] at
[te]
sides.
[Th]o   quench[tirkat]
me half way.

This moment
what is to be told?

LANGUISHING POEM

Today
I'm going to (right) a language poem
all right

First—mix up the significant signifier.
Language—lang-uag-ing on image—like
two times two equals three—2x2=3

or

blood
blood soaked
blood soaked fists
blood soaked fists reaching
blood soaked fists reaching from
blood soaked fists reaching from swastika arms
Bristling scalp
with blood soaked fists reaching brown face
ergo—face crushed beneath the onslaught.

Morrissey: London Is Dead—The National Front Disco
except
My languishing poem will be corrected.

A LEAF REVISITED

Listening vis[h]ions
smiles creeping [te] periphery
echoes quenching my land
scape
scaper slicing the mu[dh] field of rice
full of hovering mosquito pools
visions alive with the death of night.

i felt hopes soar
out of the kennel of pover[dhy].

Like white rods and flashes
they de/clare[dh] a qualitative justice
making noise and sucking out what was theirs
but t[dh]is
quiet breath
reaps not the crop I plan[tidh].
I have given myself to ooooo/blivion
As I handed my rein to a surly mast[dhe]r.

PHINDER DULAI is a freelance writer and the poetry editor for the South Asian quarterly *Ankur*. His work has been published in a number of literary magazines, including *Ankur, Canadian Ethnic Studies, the Toronto South Asian Review,* and *Rungh.* He lives in Burnaby, B.C.